In this book, we're going to talk about vectors and scalars and how they are used in physics. So, let's get right to it!

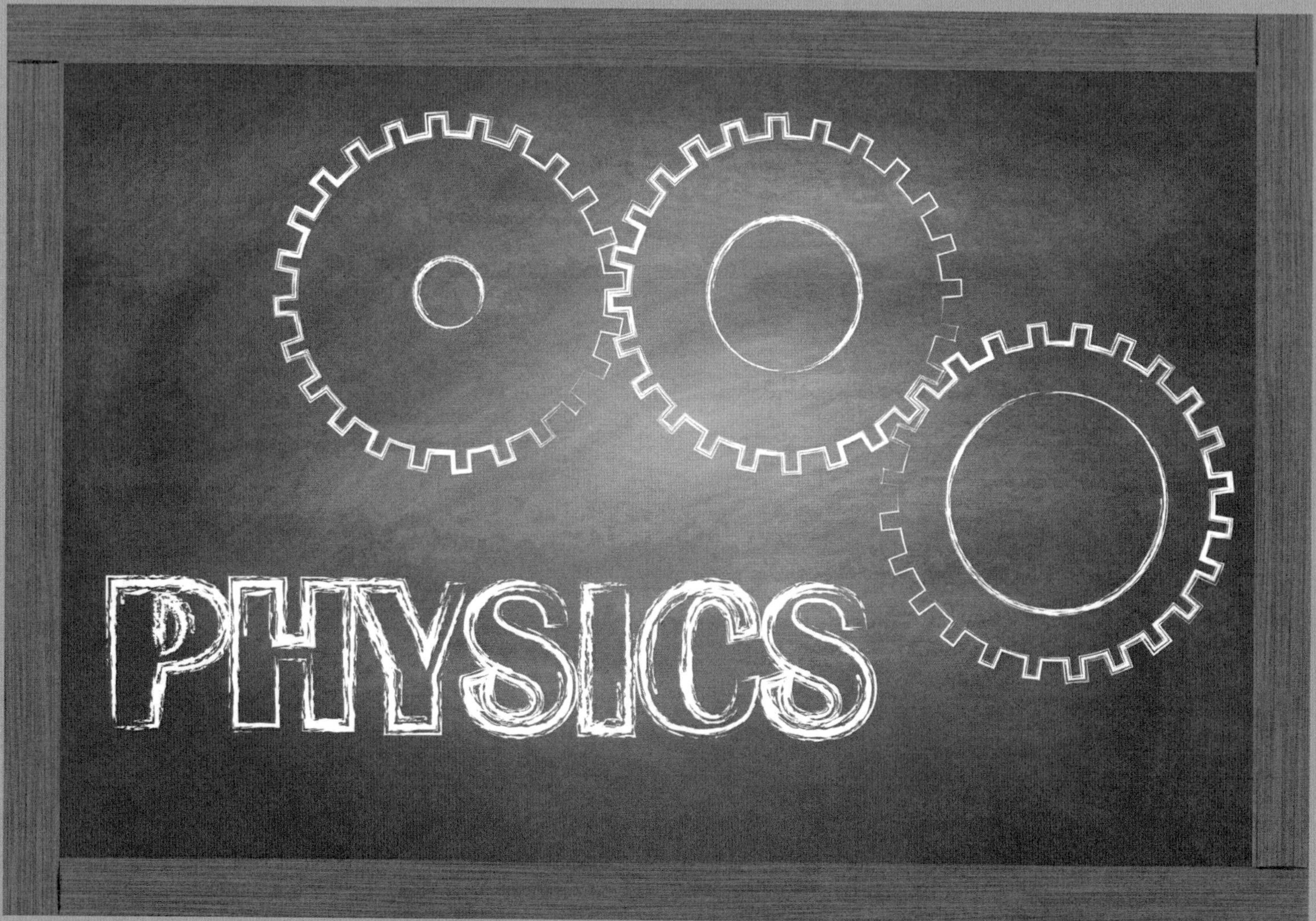
PHYSICS

The study of physics is filled with different types of measurements. Scalar quantities and vector quantities are the two different types you'll need to work with in order to solve physics problems.

WHAT IS A VECTOR?

A vector is a quantity that has more than one piece of information attached to it. It has a magnitude, which is the absolute size of a quantity. It also has a direction.

DIFFERENT PHYSICS ILLUSTRATIONS

WHAT IS A SCALAR?

The other type of quantity that is used in physics is a scalar. A scalar only has one piece of information, which is its magnitude.

EXAMPLES OF SCALAR QUANTITIES

TIME

Time doesn't have a direction. It simply has a magnitude in whatever unit of measure you give it as days, hours, minutes, or seconds.

A CLOCK

GILL PINT QUART GALLON

VOLUME MEASUREMENTS

VOLUME

Volume is the amount of space an object occupies. If you want to measure the volume of a tin can or the volume of the Earth, these volume measurements have magnitude and can be measured with lots of different units. Volume doesn't have a direction attached to it, so it is scalar.

TEMPERATURE

As long as you're not measuring any change in the temperature, then the temperature measurement is a scalar. For example, if someone asks you what temperature it is outdoors today, then your answer might be 85 degrees Fahrenheit and that's a scalar. However, if the person asked you how much of a change or delta there was from yesterday's temperature compared to today's, then that measurement will be a vector since it will be a measurement of change. In this case, that change will represent a specific direction, either up for an increase or down for a decrease.

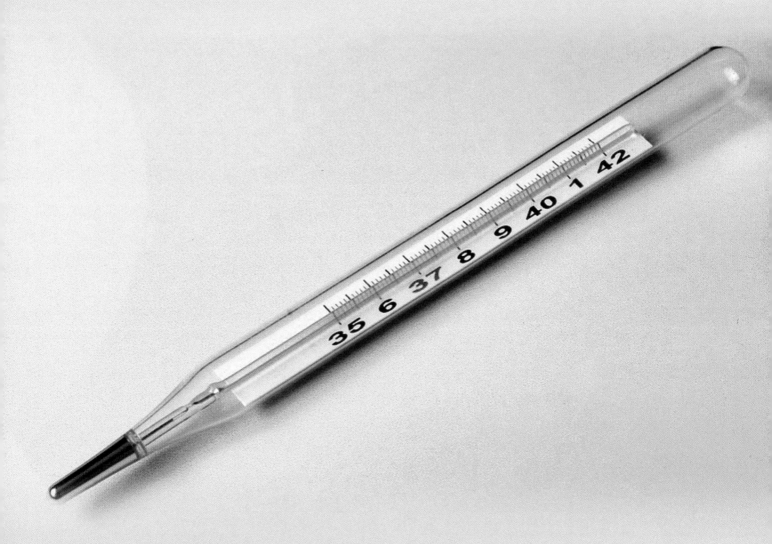

A THERMOMETER IS A DEVICE USED IN MEASURING BODY TEMPERATURE.

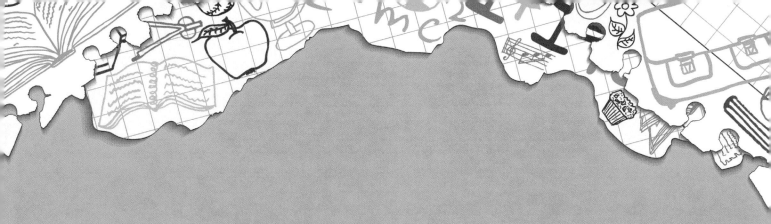

DISTANCE

If you said: "I walked 5 miles" then that distance would be scalar since you didn't tell us anything about the direction you walked. You don't necessarily have to tell us the direction. However, if you said: "I walked 5 miles southwest and then walked 10 miles east from that position" this statement would have to be represented using two vectors.

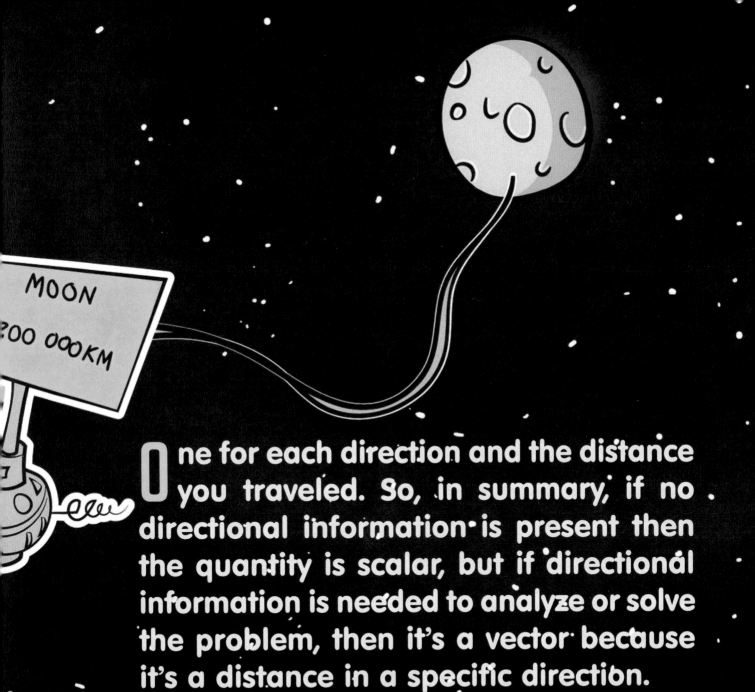

One for each direction and the distance you traveled. So, in summary, if no directional information is present then the quantity is scalar, but if directional information is needed to analyze or solve the problem, then it's a vector because it's a distance in a specific direction.

SPEEDOMETER

SPEED

Let's say you're traveling in a car and you're going 45 miles per hour. That's a scalar since you are not indicating a direction. However, if you said that you were beginning your travels from Austin, Texas and traveling 45 miles per hour in a westward direction, then that measurement, called the velocity, is a vector since it indicates direction. Speed and velocity are often mixed up when they used for measurements but they are not the same. Speed is a scalar quantity, while velocity is a vector.

WORK

Work is defined as force times displacement when the direction of both the force and displacement are the same. If the force and displacement are not the same direction, then the angle between them must be used in the calculation to get the final result for work. Notice that force and displacement are both vector quantities, but work is not. One of the reasons is that the force and displacement may not be in the same direction. Based on that, work doesn't have a direction, so it's scalar. It's actually always true that the product of two vectors yields a scalar.

THERE IS WORK WHEN YOU DROP YOUR PENCIL. IT'S BECAUSE THE DISPLACEMENT OF THE BALL FROM YOUR HAND TO THE GROUND IS GREATER THAN ZERO AND IT IS ALSO IN THE SAME DIRECTION AS THE FORCE ON THE BALL.

MASS VS. WEIGHT

MASS

The mass of an object is its density times its volume. This is a scalar quantity and doesn't vary. People confuse mass and weight all the time. One way to think about it is that the mass of an object doesn't change with gravity, but its weight does. For example, an object that has a mass of 1 kilogram, will have that same mass on Earth or on the Moon.

EXAMPLES OF VECTOR QUANTITIES

INCREASE OR DECREASE IN TEMPERATURE

A change in temperature conveys a direction either up or down so this change or delta would be described using a vector.

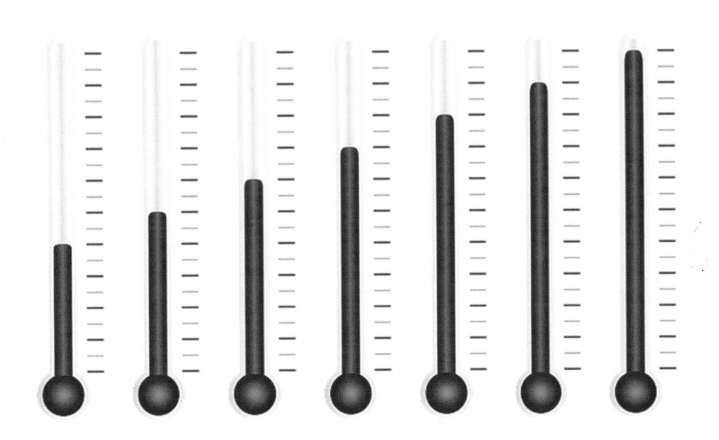

DIFFERENT TEMPERATURES

CAR RACING

VELOCITY

Velocity is the rate of change from one position to another in a specific direction. In other words, it's the rate of change of an object's displacement. For example, the car traveled from St. Petersburg, Florida to Tampa, Florida due north at 55 miles per hour.

FORCE

When you apply a force, it's in a specific direction, so it's a vector.

DISPLACEMENT

Displacement is the change from one position to another in a specific direction, so it's a vector.

WEIGHT

We don't use it this way often but weight is actually a vector. The reason is that your weight can vary depending on gravity. Your weight on Earth is due to the direction and force of gravity and would be different if you were standing on the Moon.

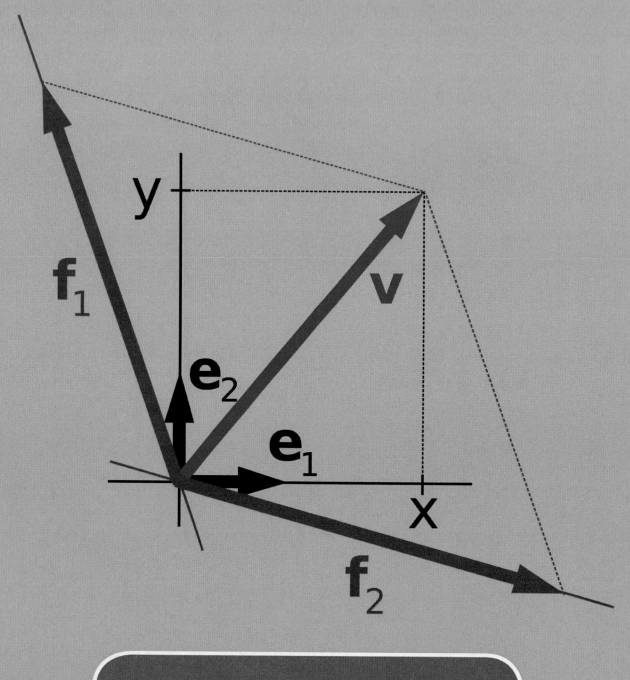

AN EXAMPLE OF VECTOR

HOW TO DRAW A VECTOR

If you are solving a problem on a piece of paper and are using a vector to indicate a specific direction, you would draw an arrow with a head and a tail so that it's clear what direction it's traveling. The arrowhead will point in the direction the vector represents. The length of the vector you draw will represent its magnitude.

HOW TO WRITE A VECTOR

When scientists or mathematicians write a vector in a formula they either use a bold letter or they place an arrow over the letter to indicate that the quantity has a direction and is a vector.

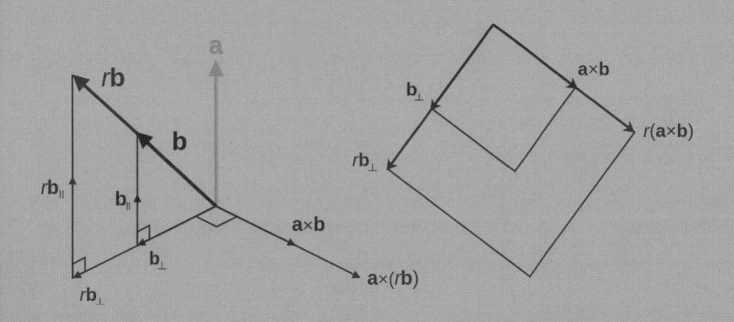

EXAMPLE OF A SCALAR VERSUS A VECTOR

Let's use an example to see how this works. Suppose you're inside a house and you're asked to measure the temperature in each room. You go to the living room and you measure the temperature there and it's 70 degrees Fahrenheit. The temperature is a scalar measurement since it only has a magnitude. You don't need a direction to describe the temperature.

Now you go into another room and you measure the temperature again. This time the temperature is 75 degrees Fahrenheit. Once again, the temperature is just a single piece of information that measures the number of degrees. The temperature is a scalar.

Other types of measurements that would be scalar are mass or power or electrical charge. Some of these types of measurements, temperature is one of them, can be negative values, but they still don't have a direction attached to them.

The temperature throughout the house isn't the same even though the thermostat has been set at 70 degrees. So, now we're wondering whether there's something wrong with the air flow in this room. In order to measure the air flow, which is really the air velocity in this room, I need to determine whether the air is moving to the right, to the left, or up and down.

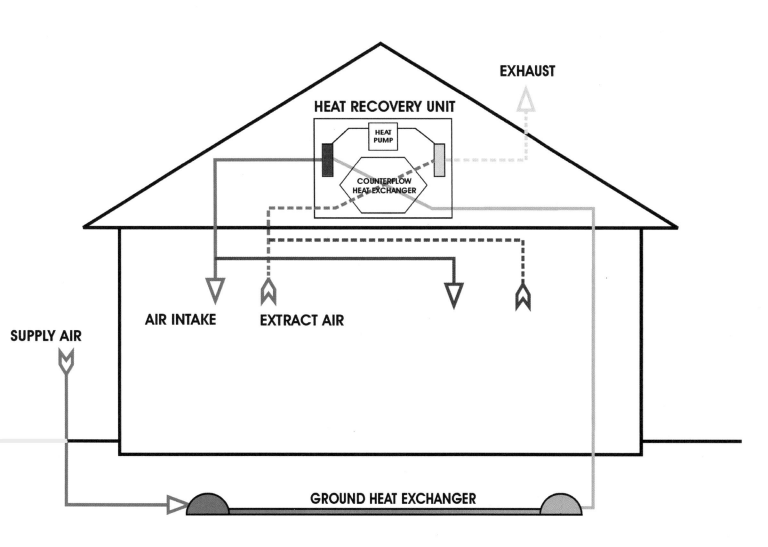

EXHAUST

HEAT RECOVERY UNIT

HEAT PUMP

COUNTERFLOW HEAT EXCHANGER

AIR INTAKE

EXTRACT AIR

SUPPLY AIR

GROUND HEAT EXCHANGER

HEAT RECOVERY VENTILATION OF A HOUSE

In other words, the air flow can be described using a measurement in 3-dimensional space or on a 3-dimensional coordinate system. The x-axis is positioned horizontally in a plane, the y-axis is positioned vertically in a plane, and the z-axis is sticking up at a right angle to the x-y plane.

To imagine how this looks, take a piece of paper and draw an x-y coordinate system on it and then put a pencil or a straw straight out of the page and perpendicular to the origin. This is the x-y-z coordinate system that represents 3-dimensional space.

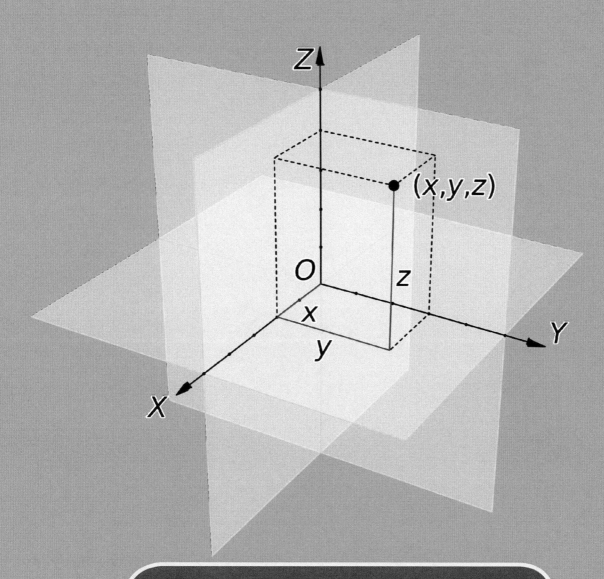

ILLUSTRATION SHOWING ITS COORDINATES

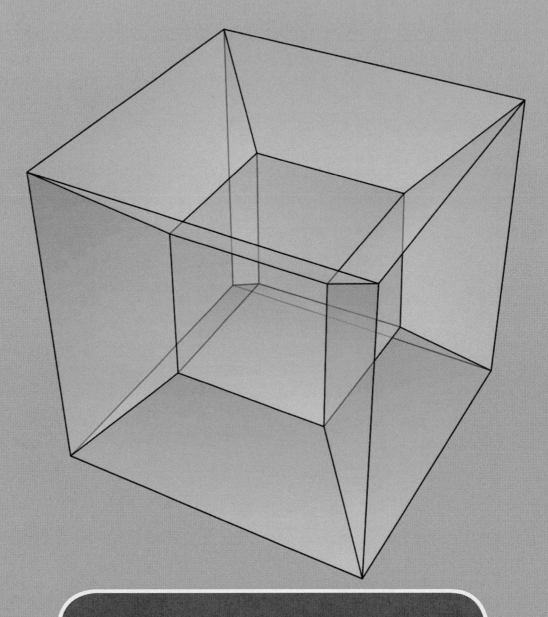

3 DIMENSIONAL OBJECT

THE FOURTH DIMENSION

We live in an environment that is 3-dimensional but vectors can be used to solve problems in dimensions that may exist but that we can't see.

SAMPLE STATEMENTS:
IS IT A VECTOR OR IS IT A SCALAR?

- The temperature today is 45 degrees Fahrenheit. This measurement is a scalar because it doesn't have a direction.

- The car traveled 60 miles per hour southeast. This measurement represents the velocity of the car and is a vector because it provides the car's direction.

- **The mass of the object in the east corner of the room is 5 kilograms. This one is tricky. The east corner has nothing to do with the mass of the object. Mass is a scalar.**

- **Stephen pedaled on his bicycle at 7 miles per hour. This measurement is the speed that Stephen is traveling, but it doesn't tell you his direction so it's scalar.**

FASCINATING FACTS ABOUT SCALARS AND VECTORS

William Rowan, who was a physicist in Ireland, first used the notation to describe a vector quantity.

Vectors can be used to describe problems in two-dimensional space. They can also be used for problems in three-dimensional space as well as dimensions that we can't yet perceive.

WILLIAM ROWAN

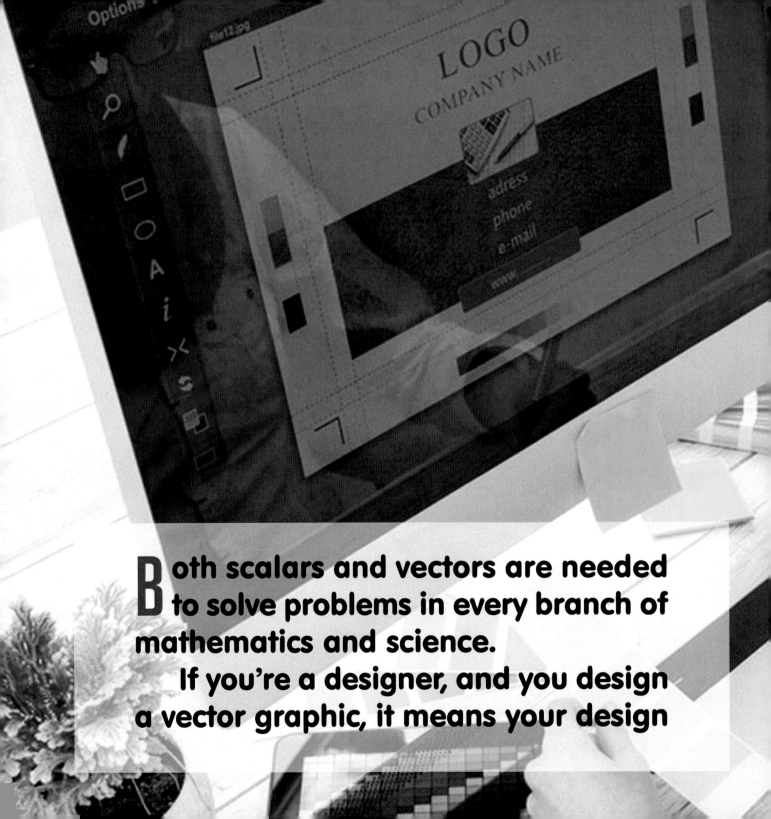

Both scalars and vectors are needed to solve problems in every branch of mathematics and science.

    If you're a designer, and you design a vector graphic, it means your design

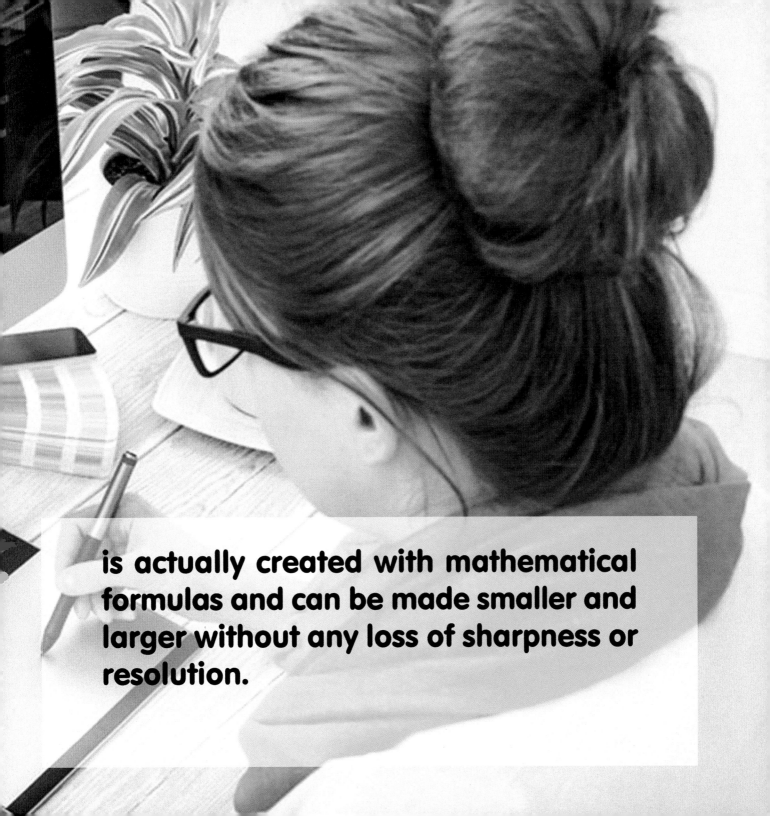

is actually created with mathematical formulas and can be made smaller and larger without any loss of sharpness or resolution.

Two different scientists, Josiah Willard Gibbs in the United States, and Oliver Heaviside of Britain, both created vector analysis independently of each other.

JAMES CLERK MAXWELL

I t was designed to explain the laws of electromagnetism that had been discovered by the famous Scottish physicist James Clerk Maxwell.

Awesome! Now you know more about how different types of measurements are used in physics. You can find more Physics books from Baby Professor by searching the website of your favorite book retailer.

Visit

BABY PROFESSOR
EDUCATION KIDS

www.BabyProfessorBooks.com
to download Free Baby Professor eBooks
and view our catalog of new and exciting
Children's Books

Made in the USA
Monee, IL
29 May 2022

97218381R00040